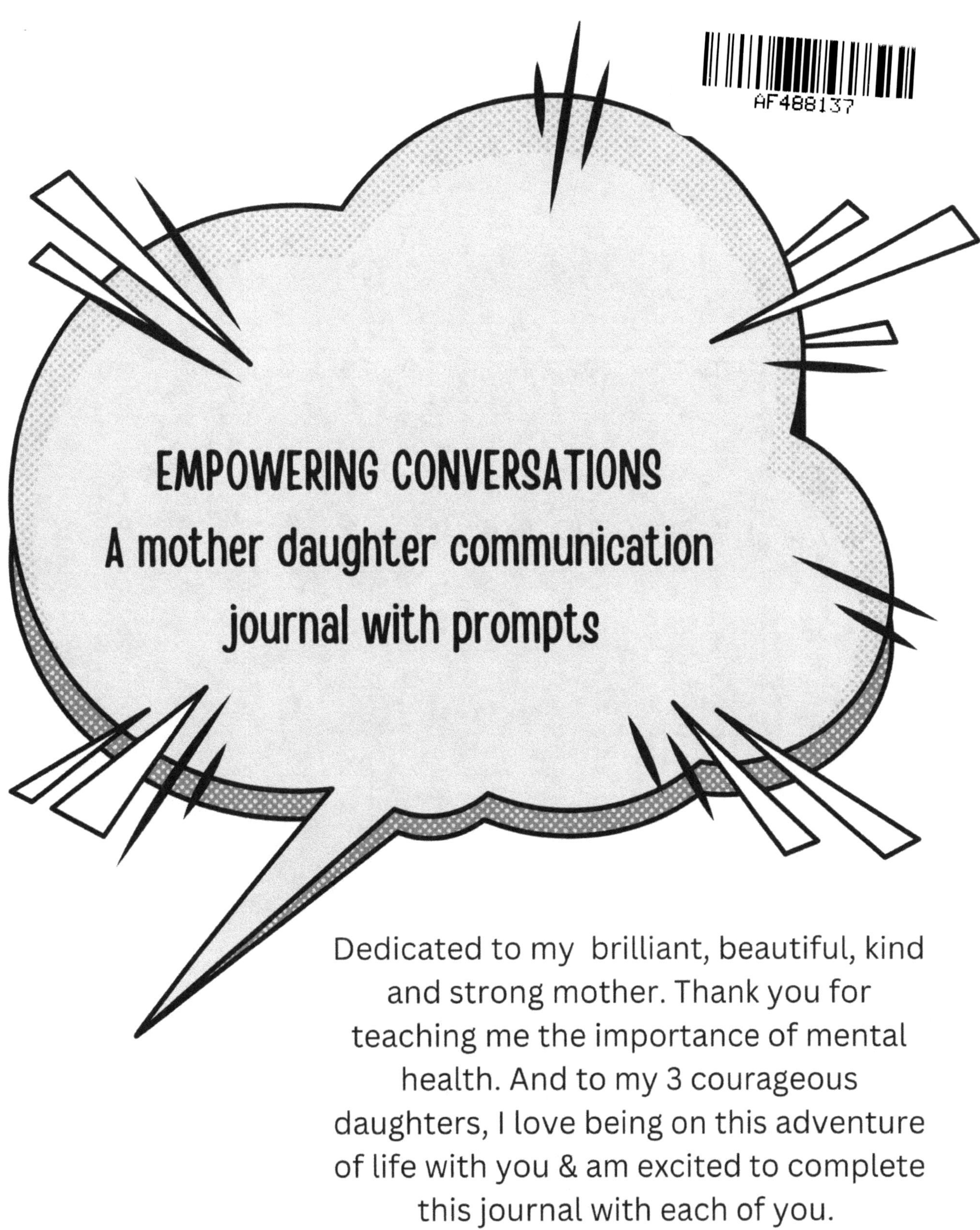

Dedicated to my brilliant, beautiful, kind and strong mother. Thank you for teaching me the importance of mental health. And to my 3 courageous daughters, I love being on this adventure of life with you & am excited to complete this journal with each of you.

MOTHER: ....

START DATE: ....

LOCATION: ....

AGE: ....

MY GOAL IN DOING THIS JOURNAL:

DAUGHTER: ....

START DATE: ....

LOCATION: ....

AGE: ....

MY GOAL IN DOING THIS JOURNAL:

Dear Daughter...

DATE ____________________

DATE ______________

Dear Daughter..
DATE

DATE ______________

DATE _______________

DATE _______________

Dear Daughter..
DATE

DATE

EMPOWERING CONVERSATION STARTERS

- WHAT MADE YOU SMILE TODAY?
- IF YOU WROTE A BOOK ABOUT YOUR LIFE, WHAT WOULD THE TITLE BE?
- IF YOU COULD DESCRIBE YOUR DREAM ADVENTURE, WHAT WOULD IT LOOK LIKE?
- WHAT IS YOUR BEST CORE MEMORY?
- WHAT IS WORK ETHIC AND WHERE CAN YOU PRACTICE IT?
- IF YOU COULD HAVE YOUR DREAM JOB WHAT WOULD IT BE?
- WHAT QUALITIES MAKE YOU A GOOD FRIEND?
- WHAT MAKES A FRIEND?
- WHAT IS TRUST?

PHOTO CREDIT: JEN COCHET

JOURNALING IDEAS

- CREATE A STORY WHERE A DAUGHTER AND A MOTHER SAVE THE WORLD.
- MAKE A TIMELINE OF YOUR LIFE.
- WRITE ABOUT YOUR FAVORITE MOTHER & DAUGHTER FROM A MOVIE.
- WRITE 5 REASONS YOU ARE GRATEFUL TO BE MY MAMA/DAUGHTER.
- ASK AN AUNT, SISTER OR FRIEND WHAT THEY LOVE MOST ABOUT OUR RELATIONSHIP.
- MAKE A LIST OF BOOKS WE COULD READ TOGETHER.
- JOURNAL FOR 10 MINUTES EVERYDAY THIS WEEK.

Dear Daughter..

DATE _______________

The love between a
mother and daughter

knows no
distance.

Dear Mama..

Dear Daughter..

DATE

DATE ______________

DATE

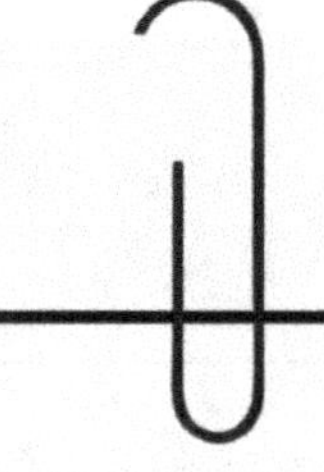

EMPOWERING CONVERSATION
JOURNALING STARTERS

- CREATE A GRAPHIC NOVEL OF OUR MOTHER DAUGHTER RELATIONSHIP.
- MAKE AN ACROSTIC POEM WITH YOUR NAME.
- WRITE ALL THE PLACES WE HAVE TRAVELED TOGETHER.
- WRITE A MOTHER DAUGHTER JOKE.
- JOURNAL IN YOUR FAVORITE SPOT TO "RELAX" IN THE HOUSE.
- MAKE A LIST OF TOP 10 THINGS YOU WOULD LIKE TO ACCOMPLISH TOGETHER.
- JOURNAL IN ALL DIFFERENT COLORS.

DATE ______________

Dear Daughter..

DATE ________________

DATE ___________________

Dear Daughter..

DATE ___________

DATE

Dear Daughter..

DATE ___________

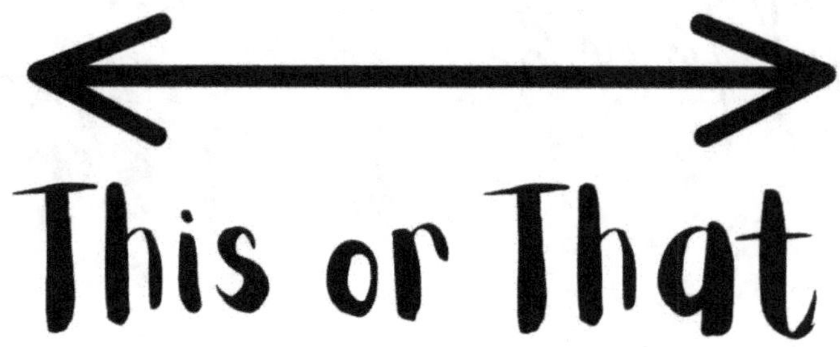

This or That

A Daughter's Point of View

Questions	Answers
Summer or Winter	______________________
Mountains or Beach	______________________
Big City or Small Town	______________________
Homework or Chores	______________________
Hot or Cold	______________________
Cake or Ice cream	______________________
Movies or Video games	______________________
Morning or Night	______________________
Dogs or Cats	______________________
Reading or TV	______________________

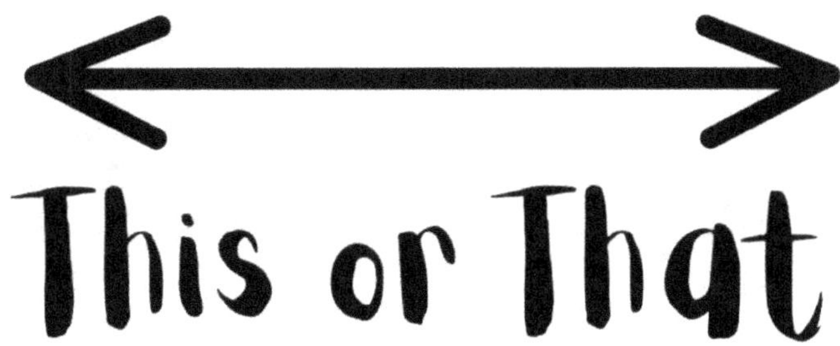

This or That

A Mama's Point of View

Questions

Summer or Winter

Mountains or Beach

Big City or Small Town

Coffee or Tea

Hot or Cold

Cake or Ice cream

Movies or Video games

Morning or Night

Dogs or Cats

Reading or TV

Answers

____

____

____

____

____

____

____

____

____

____

MY SELF PORTRAIT

My name is:________________

MY SELF PORTRAIT

A FEW OF MY FAVORITE THINGS

A Daughter's Version

A FEW OF MY FAVORITE THINGS

A Mama's Version

A DAUGHTER'S POSITIVE REFLECTIONS

What do I love about my life right now?

What do I love about myself?

What is a happy memory?

The world is a good place because...

Something fun I am looking forward to learning with you.

What I love about you.

A MAMA'S POSITIVE REFLECTIONS

What do I love about my life right now?

What do I love about myself?

What is a happy memory?

The world is a good place because...

Something fun I am looking forward to learning with you.

What I love about you.

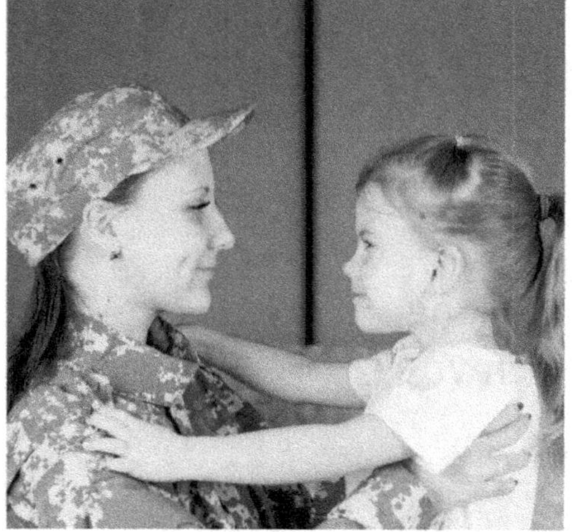

Thank you for loving me well.

ABOUT TODAY:

3 AWESOME THINGS ABOUT MY DAY

3 HARD THINGS ABOUT MY DAY

ABOUT TODAY:

3 AWESOME THINGS ABOUT MY DAY

3 HARD THINGS ABOUT MY DAY

ABOUT TODAY:

3 AWESOME THINGS ABOUT MY DAY

3 HARD THINGS ABOUT MY DAY

ABOUT TODAY:

3 AWESOME THINGS ABOUT MY DAY

3 HARD THINGS ABOUT MY DAY

ABOUT TODAY:

3 AWESOME THINGS ABOUT MY DAY

3 HARD THINGS ABOUT MY DAY

YES
GIRL!
YOU
CAN!

ABOUT TODAY:

3 AWESOME THINGS ABOUT MY DAY

3 HARD THINGS ABOUT MY DAY

ABOUT TODAY:

3 AWESOME THINGS ABOUT MY DAY

3 HARD THINGS ABOUT MY DAY

ABOUT TODAY:

3 AWESOME THINGS ABOUT MY DAY

3 HARD THINGS ABOUT MY DAY

ABOUT TODAY:

3 AWESOME THINGS ABOUT MY DAY

3 HARD THINGS ABOUT MY DAY

ABOUT TODAY:

3 AWESOME THINGS ABOUT MY DAY

3 HARD THINGS ABOUT MY DAY

ABOUT TODAY:

3 AWESOME THINGS ABOUT MY DAY

3 HARD THINGS ABOUT MY DAY

PHOTO CREDIT BEN MASORA

WAYS YOU CAN PRAY FOR ME

WAYS YOU CAN PRAY FOR ME

WAYS YOU CAN PRAY FOR ME

WAYS YOU CAN PRAY FOR ME

WAYS YOU CAN PRAY FOR ME

I feel empowered when.......

I feel empowered when.......

I feel empowered when.......

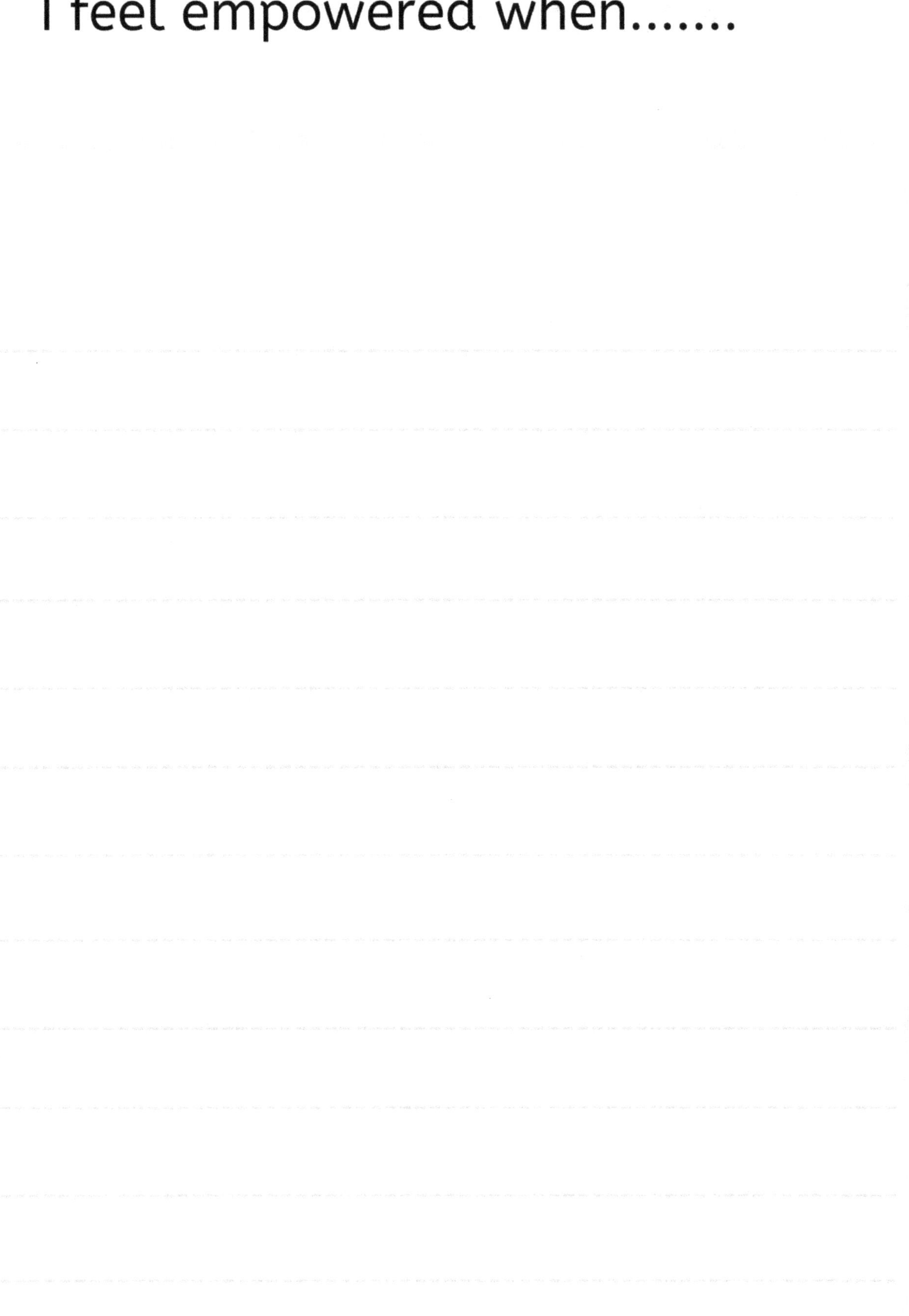

I feel empowered when.......

I feel empowered when.......

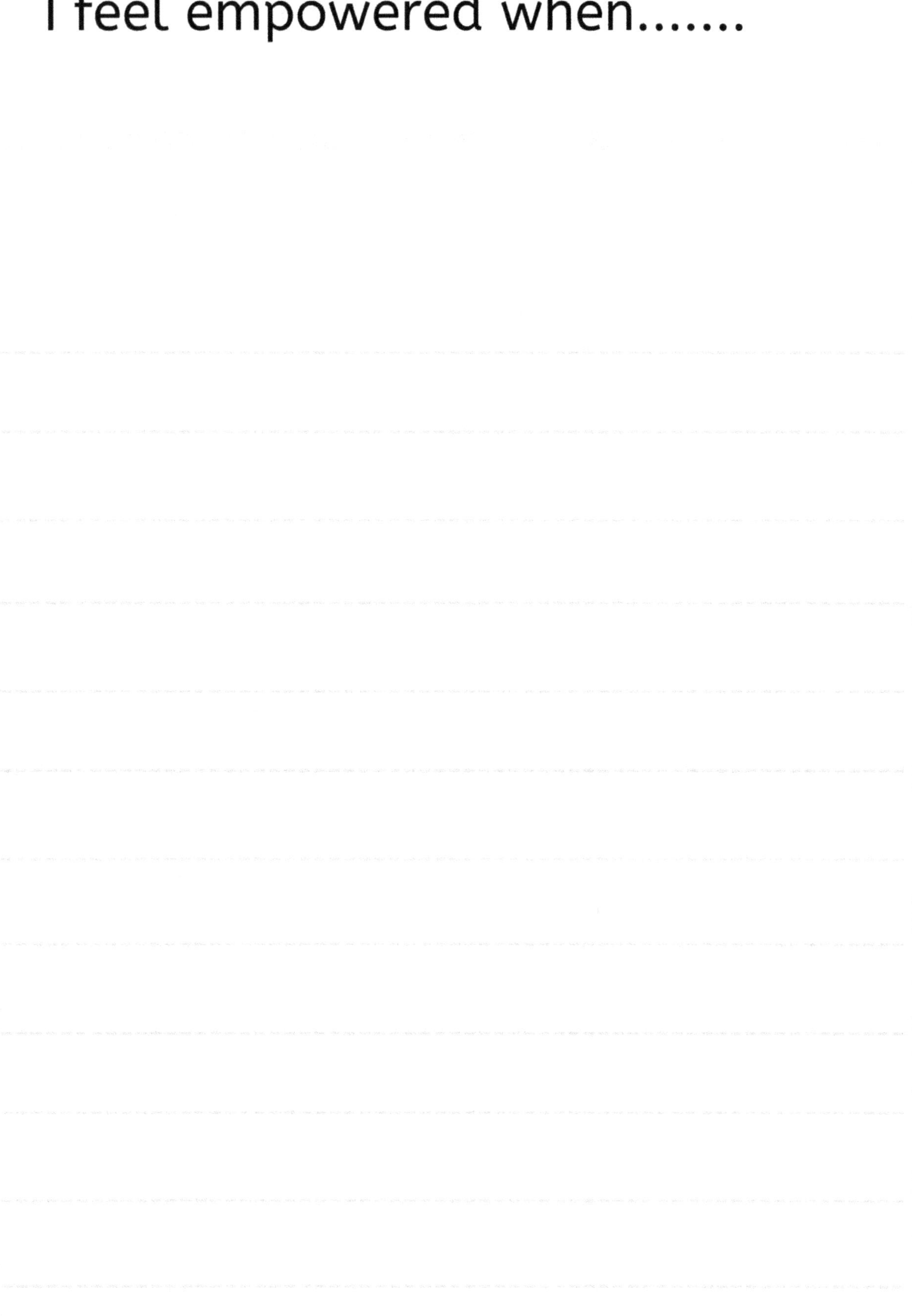

I feel empowered when.......

I feel empowered when.......

Women in our Family

FAMILY NAME:

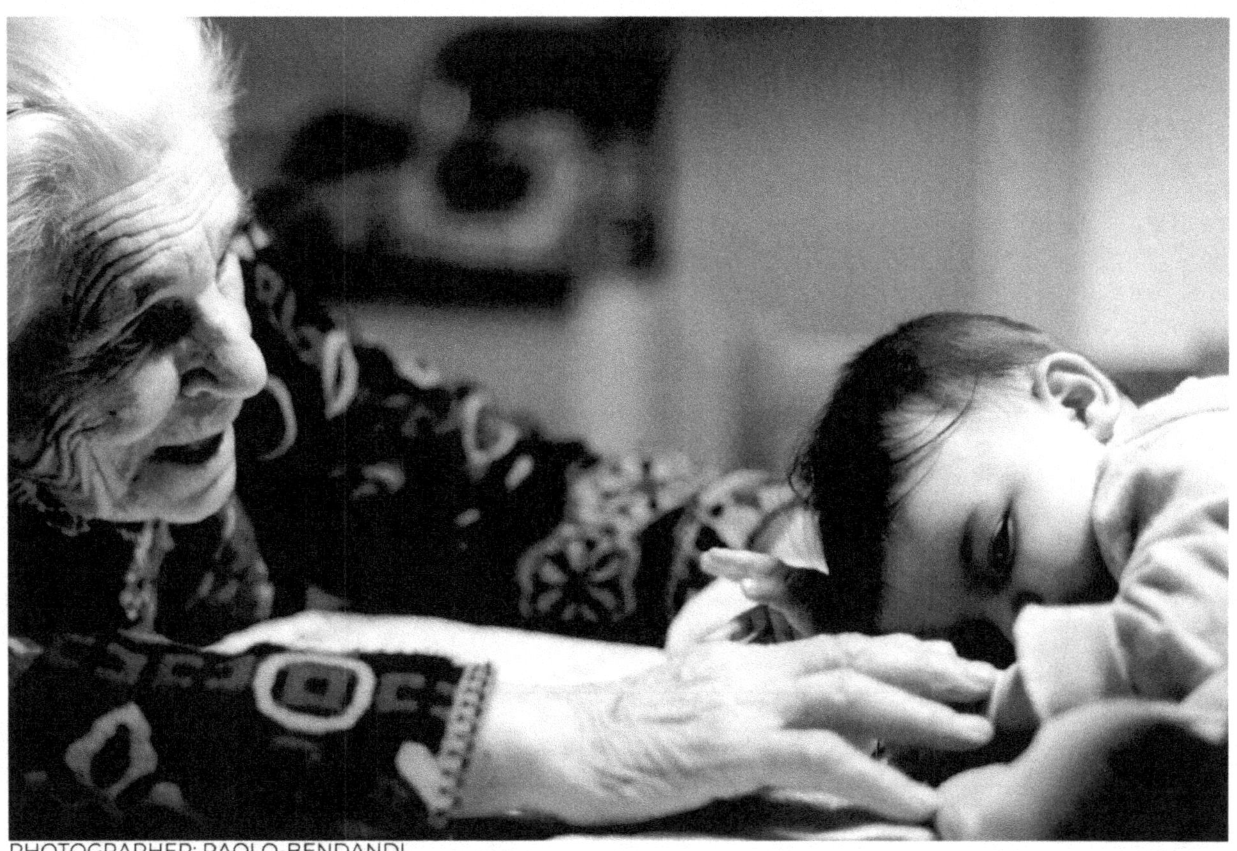

PHOTOGRAPHER: PAOLO-BENDANDI

Family Recipe

NAME OF DISH

FROM THE KITCHEN OF

INGREDIENTS

SERVES

PREP TIME

TOTAL TIME

OVEN TEMP

DIRECTIONS

Family Recipe

NAME OF DISH

FROM THE KITCHEN OF

INGREDIENTS

SERVES

PREP TIME

TOTAL TIME

OVEN TEMP

DIRECTIONS

Family Recipe

NAME OF DISH

FROM THE KITCHEN OF

INGREDIENTS

SERVES

PREP TIME

TOTAL TIME

OVEN TEMP

DIRECTIONS

PHOTO CREDIT: CHRISTIAN BOWEN

Family Recipe

NAME OF DISH

FROM THE KITCHEN OF

INGREDIENTS

SERVES

PREP TIME

TOTAL TIME

OVEN TEMP

DIRECTIONS

Family Recipe

NAME OF DISH

FROM THE KITCHEN OF

INGREDIENTS

SERVES

PREP TIME

TOTAL TIME

OVEN TEMP

DIRECTIONS

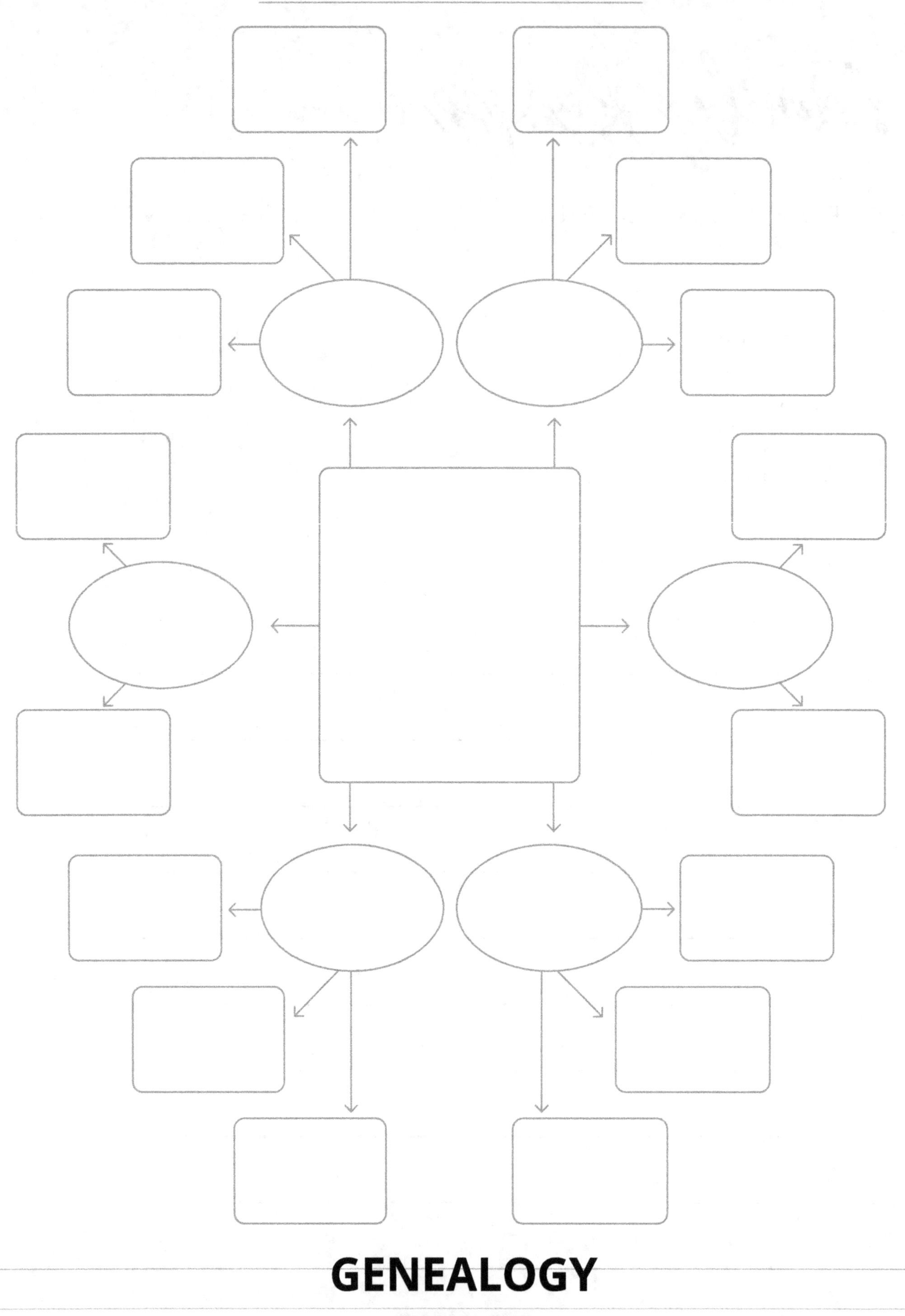

GENEALOGY
CHART

MY SUCCESSES

The accomplishment I am most proud of is.....

How I felt when I began.....

How I felt when I was in the process.....

How I felt when I accomplished it.....

MY SUCCESSES

The accomplishment I am most proud of is.....

How I felt when I began.....

How I felt when I was in the process.....

How I felt when I accomplished it.....

MY SUCCESSES

The accomplishment I am most proud of is.....

How I felt when I began.....

How I felt when I was in the process.....

How I felt when I accomplished it.....

LESSONS LEARNED

I learned a lot when I made this choice...

How I felt when I began to realize I failed.....

How I felt in the process of learning from this.....

How I felt when I got back up again.....

LESSONS LEARNED

I learned a lot when I made this choice...

How I felt when I began to realize I failed.....

How I felt in the process of learning from this.....

How I felt when I got back up again.....

LESSONS LEARNED

I learned a lot when I made this choice...

How I felt when I began to realize I failed.....

How I felt in the process of learning from this.....

How I felt when I got back up again.....

SOMETIMES YOU WIN

SOMETIMES YOU LEARN

QUIZ

GOOD SELF ESTEEM HELPS YOU TO HAVE WHAT AROUND OTHERS?

A.	CONFIDENCE	C.	MOOD SWINGS
B.	OPTIMISM	D	SELF-CONCEPT

HAVING A POSITIVE ATTITUDE TOWARDS YOUR FUTURE, MEANS THAT YOU ARE...

A.	RESILIENT	C.	OPTIMISTIC
B.	VIBING	D	CONFIDENT

SELF-AWARENESS INCLUDES KNOWING ABOUT MY...

A.	STRENGTHS	C.	HOBBIES
B.	WEAKNESSES	D	ALL OF THE ABOVE

WHAT IS A "NEED"?

A.	A BOAT	C.	FOOD
B.	FLOWERS	D	CLOTHES

PHOTO CREDIT: CAOLINE HERNANDEZ

Mental health check up

DATE _______________________

HOW ARE YOU FEELING TODAY?

WHAT HAVE BEEN YOUR THREE DOMINANT EMOTIONS THIS WEEK?

○ _______________________
○ _______________________
○ _______________________

HOW HAVE YOU MANAGED YOUR FEELINGS?

HOW ARE YOU FEELING TODAY?

HOW CAN YOU IMPROVE YOUR MENTAL HEALTH?

THINGS THAT TRIGGER ME:

○ _______________________
○ _______________________
○ _______________________
○ _______________________

MY RANKING OF MY MENTAL HEALTH THIS WEEK

☆ ☆ ☆ ☆

Mental health check up

DATE _______________________

HOW ARE YOU FEELING TODAY?

HOW ARE YOU FEELING TODAY?

HOW CAN YOU IMPROVE YOUR
MENTAL HEALTH?

WHAT HAVE BEEN YOUR THREE
DOMINANT EMOTIONS THIS WEEK?

○ _______________________

○ _______________________

○ _______________________

HOW HAVE YOU MANAGED YOUR
FEELINGS?

THINGS THAT TRIGGER ME

○ _______________________

○ _______________________

○ _______________________

○ _______________________

MY RANKING OF MY MENTAL
HEALTH THIS WEEK

☆ ☆ ☆ ☆

Mental health check up

DATE _______________

HOW ARE YOU FEELING TODAY?

HOW ARE YOU FEELING TODAY?

HOW CAN YOU IMPROVE YOUR
MENTAL HEALTH?

WHAT HAVE BEEN YOUR THREE
DOMINANT EMOTIONS THIS WEEK?

○ _______________

○ _______________

○ _______________

HOW HAVE YOU MANAGED YOUR
FEELINGS?

THINGS THAT TRIGGER ME

○ _______________

○ _______________

○ _______________

○ _______________

MY RANKING OF MY MENTAL
HEALTH THIS WEEK

☆ ☆ ☆ ☆

Mental health check up

DATE

HOW ARE YOU FEELING TODAY?

HOW ARE YOU FEELING TODAY?

HOW CAN YOU IMPROVE YOUR
MENTAL HEALTH?

WHAT HAVE BEEN YOUR THREE
DOMINANT EMOTIONS THIS WEEK?

○

○

○

HOW HAVE YOU MANAGED YOUR
FEELINGS?

THINGS THAT TRIGGER ME

○

○

○

○

MY RANKING OF MY MENTAL
HEALTH THIS WEEK

☆ ☆ ☆ ☆

Mental health check up

DATE ___________________

HOW ARE YOU FEELING TODAY?

HOW ARE YOU FEELING TODAY?

HOW CAN YOU IMPROVE YOUR
MENTAL HEALTH?

WHAT HAVE BEEN YOUR THREE
DOMINANT EMOTIONS THIS WEEK?

○ ___________________

○ ___________________

○ ___________________

HOW HAVE YOU MANAGED YOUR
FEELINGS?

THINGS THAT TRIGGER ME

○ ___________________

○ ___________________

○ ___________________

○ ___________________

MY RANKING OF MY MENTAL
HEALTH THIS WEEK

☆ ☆ ☆ ☆

Mental health check up

DATE ________________________

HOW ARE YOU FEELING TODAY?

WHAT HAVE BEEN YOUR THREE
DOMINANT EMOTIONS THIS WEEK?

○ ___________________________

○ ___________________________

○ ___________________________

HOW HAVE YOU MANAGED YOUR
FEELINGS?

HOW ARE YOU FEELING TODAY?

HOW CAN YOU IMPROVE YOUR
MENTAL HEALTH?

THINGS THAT TRIGGER ME

○ ___________________________

○ ___________________________

○ ___________________________

○ ___________________________

MY RANKING OF MY MENTAL
HEALTH THIS WEEK

☆ ☆ ☆ ☆

You are strong
and capable

30 DAYS CHALLENGE

CREATE A CHALLENGE TO TAKE ON TOGETHER

DAY 1	DAY 2	DAY 3	DAY 4	DAY 5

DAY 6	DAY 7	DAY 8	DAY 9	DAY 10

DAY 11	DAY 12	DAY 13	DAY 14	DAY 15

DAY 16	DAY 17	DAY 18	DAY 19	DAY 20

DAY 21	DAY 22	DAY 23	DAY 24	DAY 25

DAY 26	DAY 27	DAY 28	DAY 29	DAY 30

30 DAYS CHALLENGE

CREATE A CHALLENGE TO TAKE ON TOGETHER

DAY 1	DAY 2	DAY 3	DAY 4	DAY 5

DAY 6	DAY 7	DAY 8	DAY 9	DAY 10

DAY 11	DAY 12	DAY 13	DAY 14	DAY 15

DAY 16	DAY 17	DAY 18	DAY 19	DAY 20

DAY 21	DAY 22	DAY 23	DAY 24	DAY 25

DAY 26	DAY 27	DAY 28	DAY 29	DAY 30

I learn best when:

School Information

Name

Teacher

How Do You Learn Best?

Rate your learning styles from one to five stars.

Visual

Auditory

Kinesthetic

LEARNING

What can I do to help you learn?

What would you like me to know?

Favorite Things

Lunch

Book

Subject

Activity

Your Strengths

What are some of your biggest academic strengths?

Your Weaknesses

What are some of your biggest academic weaknesses?

PHOTOGRAPHER: MAREKO-TAMALEA

CONVERSATION CARDS

Who was your favorite teacher in school?

What is your favorite day of the week?

What was your favorite tv show as a child?

Who was your best friend growing up?

What is your favorite dessert?

How do you fill your cup?

Tell me a story about your childhood.

What is your favorite time of day?

Tell me about my birth.

CONVERSATION CARDS

Who is your favorite teacher in school?

What is your favorite day of the week?

What is your favorite tv show?

What quality do you look for in a friend?

What is your favorite dessert?

How do you fill your cup?

Tell me a story about my childhood.

What is your favorite time of day?

What does your YES day look like?

Photo credit: Rochelle Brown

Dear Daughter,
On the Day you were born...

<u>Dear Mama,</u>
<u>Tell me about the relationship with your</u>
<u>mother when you were growing up...</u>

Dear Mama,
Tell me about the relationship with your grandmothers...

advice and wishes

FOR MY DAUGHTER

ALWAYS

NEVER

SOMETIMES ITS BEST TO

REMEMBER THAT

DONT FORGET TO

I WISH YOU

with love

mother

noun.

A person who sees the best in you
no matter what.

Loves unconditionally and keeps
the best memories.

PHOTO CREDIT: EYE FOR EBONY

THINGS THAT I HEAR

what you say vs what I hear

"You got number 19 on the test of 20 wrong."

VS.

"You never get things right."

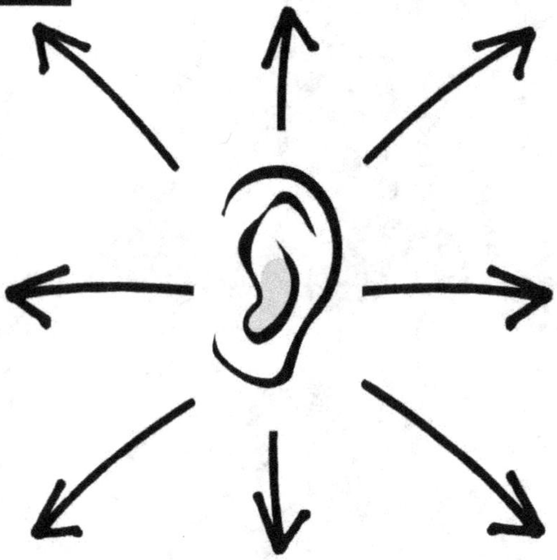

THINGS THAT I HEAR

what you say vs what I hear

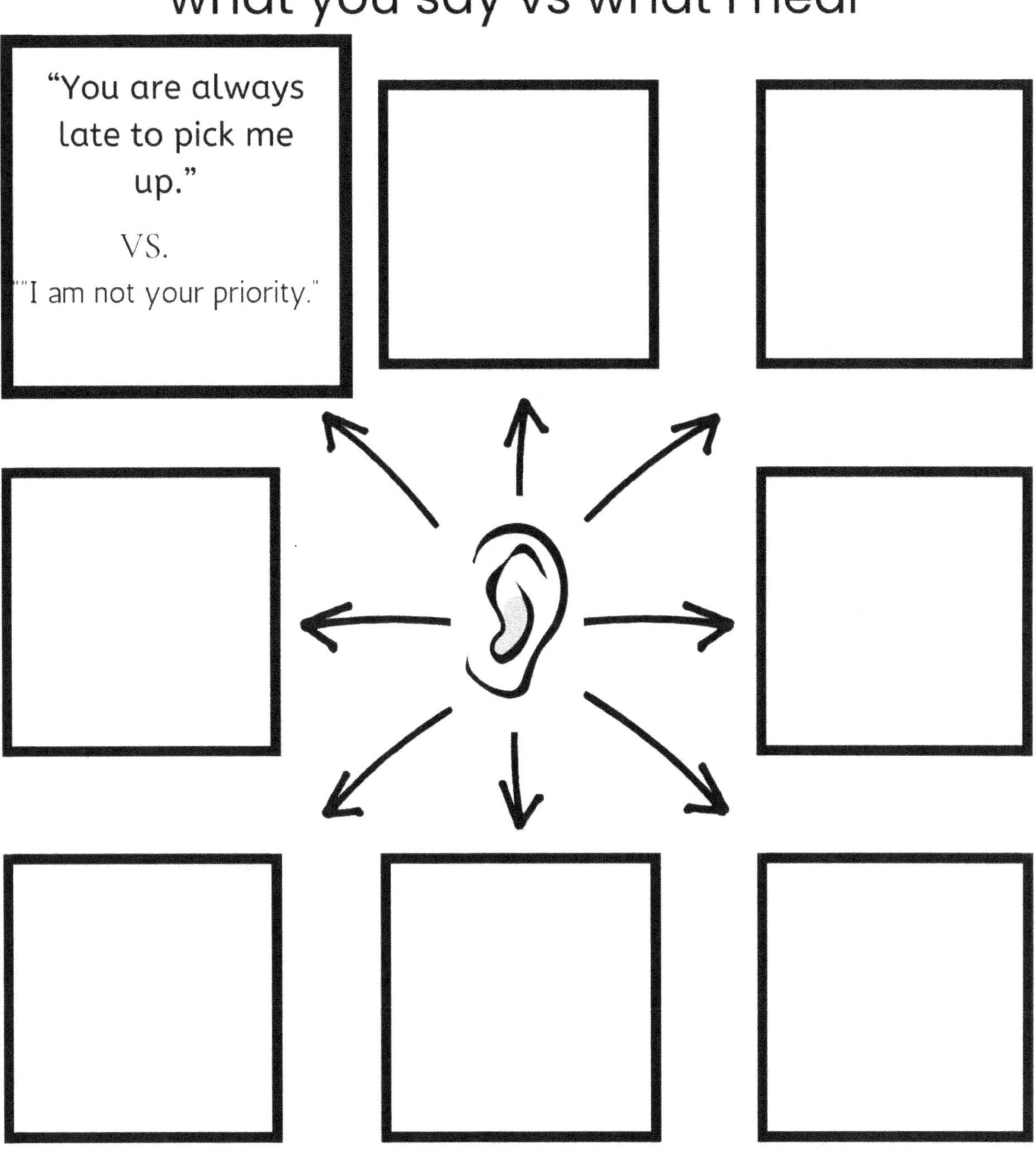

WHAT I WISH YOU KNEW

Date:

Today I am grateful for..

A Song I am loving

Sometimes it is easier to write than say....

About My Friends

Favorite Foods

WHAT I WISH YOU KNEW

Date:

Today I am grateful for

A Song I am loving

Sometimes it is easier to write than say....

About My Friends

Favorite Foods

WHAT I WISH YOU KNEW

Date: _______________

Today I am grateful for

A Song I am loving

Sometimes it is easier to write than say....

About My Friends

Favorite Foods

Photo credit: Maria Budanova

CREATE YOUR OWN
ADVENTURES OF A MOM & DAUGHTER
Graphic
NOVEL

Adventures of a Mom & Daughter
Graphic
NOVEL

Adventures of a Mom & Daughter

Graphic NOVEL

Adventures of a Mom & Daughter
Graphic
NOVEL

Adventures of a Mom & Daughter
Graphic
NOVEL

Adventures of a Mom & Daughter
Graphic
NOVEL

Adventures of a Mom & Daughter
Graphic
NOVEL
Adventures of a Mom & Daughter

Adventures of a Mom & Daughter
Graphic
NOVEL

Adventures of a Mom & Daughter
Graphic
NOVEL
Adventures of a Mom & Daughter

Adventures of a Mom & Daughter
Graphic
NOVEL

Photo Credit: Jonathan Borba

Feelings Check-in

FILL IN THE JAR WITH YOUR FEELINGS COLORS TODAY

Angry = Red	Happy = Yellow	Sad = Blue
Nervous = Purple	Excited = Green	Calm = Orange

Feelings Check-in

FILL IN THE JAR WITH YOUR FEELINGS COLORS TODAY

Angry = Red	Happy = Yellow	Sad = Blue
Nervous = Purple	Excited = Green	Calm = Orange

Feelings Check-in

FILL IN THE JAR WITH YOUR FEELINGS COLORS TODAY

Angry = Red	Happy = Yellow	Sad = Blue
Nervous = Purple	Excited = Green	Calm = Orange

Feelings Check-in

FILL IN THE JAR WITH YOUR FEELINGS COLORS TODAY

Angry = Red	Happy = Yellow	Sad = Blue
Nervous = Purple	Excited = Green	Calm = Orange

Feelings Check-in

FILL IN THE JAR WITH YOUR FEELINGS COLORS TODAY

Angry = Red	Happy = Yellow	Sad = Blue
Nervous = Purple	Excited = Green	Calm = Orange

MOTHER:

FINISH DATE:

LOCATION:

AGE:

HOW I FEEL AFTER DOING THIS JOURNAL:

DAUGHTER:

FINISH DATE:

LOCATION:

AGE:

HOW I FEEL AFTER DOING THIS JOURNAL: